This book belongs to:

A catalogue record for this book is available from the British Library
Published by Ladybird Books Ltd
80 Strand London WC2R 0RL
A Penguin Company
2 4 6 8 10 9 7 5 3 1

ISBN: 978-184646-967-1

Printed in China

First Words and Pictures

Park

illustrated by
Maria Maddocks

tree

leaf

pond

duck

flower

ant

swing

slide

roundabout

see-saw

bench

pushchair

clouds

sun

dog

ball

butterfly

ladybird

bird

feather

rain

umbrella

rainbow

puddle